Illustrated by Marie Cirillo

SEE THE BEST.
POOF THE REST.

[:)]

U. R. Moore

authorHOUSE®

AuthorHouse™
1663 Liberty Drive, Suite 200
Bloomington, IN 47403
www.authorhouse.com
Phone: 1-800-839-8640

First published by AuthorHouse 7/21/2008

ISBN: 978-1-4343-7892-7 (sc)

Library of Congress Control Number: 2008903834

Printed in the United States of America
Bloomington, Indiana

This book is printed on acid-free paper.

Foreword

Are we messing up the Original Divine Design by just reacting and keeping busy? Would it be better to pause, ask for guidance, wait and listen before we each scatter into our individual plans?

Perhaps we are like fans that enter a stadium. Finding large cards on each of our chairs, we go about rearranging the letters into what we think they should read. However, only the director of the cards can see the full design. The only way to view the outcome is not rearrange the cards at whim. When it is time, the message is visible to all within the same moment. It will be clear only by original design, not by scattered efforts.

It is with great hope that this book, "SEE THE BEST. POOF THE REST. *[:)]*" will offer non-denominational insights into clearing our energy playing field, with the intention of being ready for the Original Design to play out in full.

Contents

Chapter 1

The lessons on manifestation are all around us today.

Look online for TheSecret.tv, AbrahamHicks. com, Masteringalchemy.com, and even Pranichealing.com. Many of these websites offer free downloads and have free mp3 downloads or meditations. Feel free to check them out and enjoy a new talent of manifestation in your life. This book uses several manifestation skills and adds texting as a new tool to focus powerful emotional thoughts in our everyday lives. This book is huge. When you get it, you have it all. *[:)]*

The most important concept is that UR>. That is to say (UR>) you are more than. (Not used as you are greater than, since that has a different connotation online.) You are more than you understand.

To read or think this is not enough.
Know this is so.
Believe this is so.

UR> = you are more than
UR> your body.
UR> your house, car, or bank account.
UR> your clothes,
even if you think
they make the man/woman/child.
UR> your family, friends,
groups, associates, fame.

UR>.
Believe it.

The interesting fact is that UR> whether you wish to be or not. UR> whether you believe it or not. Since you are more than you know, you are manifesting all the time without conscious awareness of it. After a time we look back on our lives and question, "How did I get here?" The answer, my friend, is by every emotional thought, word and deed. If you are somewhere that is not to your liking, remember UR> and choose again. If you do not like what you are playing out, simply rewrite it. You choose your own adventure. Act 1 is over. Let Act 2 begin.

Chapter 2

UR> (you are more than) because you are part of a Divine Ocean.

Some say we are spiritual beings on this human journey. Others say we have a Higher Soul guiding us. Still others feel we live many lifetimes and evolve through each one. Many of the holy books speak of this. See the holy book of your choosing for more details.

Think of it this way:

We are living in a huge Divine Ocean. You are in fact like a cup of this Divine Ocean. This Ocean consists of the good and the not so good. Each cup/soul has the essence of the Divine Ocean, but is by itself not the whole of the Ocean. Without any one soul, this Ocean is incomplete.

[:)] U. R. Moore

A good way to look at this
might be that
X + U =
all the power in the universe.

An image of a small part of this (X) Divine Ocean may look like this:

[:)] [ur]> *[:)]* [ur]> *[:)]* [ur]>

[:)] [ur]> *[:)]* [ur]> *[:)]* [ur]>

[ur]>*[:)]* [ur]> *[:)]* *[:)]*

You are one of these images.

However, without you it looks like this:

[:)] [ur]> *[:)]* [ur]> *[:)]* [ur]>

[:)] [ur]> *[:)]* [ur]> *[:)]* [ur]>

[:)] [ur]> void *[:)]* The Divine Ocean goes on and on, but has a void without you, or any one soul.

This book attempts to show you that (UR>) you are more than you may understand right now. That by being part of this Divine Ocean, each of us has qualities of that Ocean. One quality is manifestation. We manifest in our lives with every emotional thought we have. This happens weather we want it to or not, weather we know it or not. It is like a boomerang effect; we get back to us exactly what we think about... Simple? Maybe. The problem is that we are doing this unconsciously and leaving boomerang messes as we go.

Begin to understand HOW IMPORTANT YOU ARE.

Begin to understand HOW IMPORTANT I AM.

Begin to understand HOW IMPORTANT EACH ONE IS, INCLUDING THE GOOD AND THE NOT SO GOOD.

Ask your personal image of the Divine for help and guidance. In my humble opinion, the name you choose is unimportant. A rose by any other name is just as sweet. However, intention is everything. We are creating by our every emotional thought, word and deed. This is so if we want to create or not.

What if we were
more
conscious
and
mindful?

We created whatever mess we see. Perhaps this can help clean up in some small way.

The Divine Ocean image works for me, but perhaps an image of a puzzle works better for you. Think how frustrating it is to complete a puzzle consisting of all the universes that exist, but missing that one single piece. Alternatively, perhaps the other image is of a puzzle piece that is not self-contained and is squishy. It either oozes onto other pieces around it or melts without holding its own placement.

The main idea is that you are more important than you know. When you step into the knowingness of how important you truly are your life will change. For me that change happened within hours. Enjoy this journey. It is fun, interesting, challenging and, I think, the main reason for our being here.

It would be wonderful to hear about your journey. Please share it with me. ENJOY.

Chapter 3

KISSES

Control your thinking and you control your world. Emotional thought literally creates a boomerang effect. Your emotional thoughts come right back to you. So be very careful what you think about, it will come about and kiss you or bite you.

Using the acronym K.I.S.S.E.S.

1. KEEP IT SIMPLE

2. Inhale White Light

3. See the best

4. Smile with gratitude

5. Exhale as you poof the rest

6. Shine

Keep it simple. Words can be divisive. Try putting a clear mental image in a frame. Words are useful to divide, separate, and identify. A picture or text message can be easier and create clearer intent. Create a mental image of a very simple picture or text message. Put this image in a frame.

Inhale beautiful White Light into your framed image. Think of the White Light as the essence of the Divine Energy in whatever form that means to you.

See it clearly. This White Light makes your framed image into a virtual movie. It transforms it into the best-of-the-best-of-the-best, situation for everyone concerned.

Smile with gratitude because each emotional thought is creating more of the same in your life. Gratitude's boomerang effect is that more of exactly what you want comes right back into your life. So smile. Smile often. Smile with reason. Smile without reason. Just smile and send that energy into your future repeatedly. (Note that this one tool will shift your very existence within a short time.)

Exhale and see the White Light swirl in your framed image. Make the light crystal clear and pull every ounce of negativity out of the framed image. At that instant, everything outside your framed image will burst into spectacular fireworks. These fireworks poof away all the rest. The intention is to poof away all doubts, fears, questions, and obstacles. Poof be gone to all ands, ifs, and buts.

Shine as you now see your clear framed image with blessings and clarity. You have now sent the energy of this framed image into your future. If you have used the acronym KISSES, this energy will have a boomerang effect of a kiss. If there is any negative energy placed into your framed image, it will have a boomerang effect and bite you. Think of this with a bully. Bless the bully and the boomerang effects will be a kiss to the one blessing and a bite to the bully. Relax; the universe is a balanced system. Just learn the rules of the game.

Summary:

Keeping it simple, create a framed image [ ].

Inhale White Light into the framed image.

See: it clearly as it changes into a virtual movie.

Watch it as you see the best it can possibly be.

Smile) with gratitude.

Exhale as you poof all the rest in spectacular fireworks*. Let it all go.

Shine. The final image of See the best, Poof the rest is now *[:)]*.

Chapter 4

Shine

Now that we can use KISSES to create and re-create in our own lives, the last step is to Shine. Our framed image is a great tool to send positive energy into the future. We now have skills to create even more. We now can Poof with the intention of clearing the gap between yours *[:)]*, mine *[:)]*, and ours *[:)]***[:)]*.

Let's take this image of the
Divine Ocean wave of our universe:

[:)] [ur]> *[:)]* [ur]> *[:)]* [ur]>

[:)] [ur]> *[:)]* [ur]> *[:)]* [ur]>

and see the best, poof the rest *[:)]*.

Now the image includes, but is not limited to, clearing the gaps between every one of us. The Divine Ocean infuses with spectacular fireworks clearing negative energies of all kinds.

The next question is a question of timing.
Since time is
in and of itself
an illusion,
the only real time is
NOW.
Does it matter when we each do this?
Would it be more effective if at 12 noon our
local time we each take one minute to do
this intention?
I know I do not know,
but I can allow for the wisdom greater then
I to take this wheel on this Divinely inspired
journey.

Chapter 5

Unseen helpers

Unseen helpers are all around us all of our days here. Ask for guidance. I truly believe that we have free will here. I further believe that if we do ask, a multitude of unseen helpers answer our call. If we refuse to ask for their help, I see them standing around with dusty wings. So ask for help. The answers will come. Just like the mall scene in the movie The Minority Report. "ASK. WAIT. WAIT. WAIT." You will receive messages in dreams, music and coincidences.

An image of you [ur]>, plus an image of an angel (or any positive unseen helper you prefer) ~ {} ~, plus an image of me *[:)]* together may look something like this:

[ur]> ~ {} ~ *[:)]* ~ {} ~ [ur]> ~ {} ~

[:)] ~ {} ~ [**ur**]> ~ {} ~ *[:)]* ~ {} ~ and the Divine Ocean wave of our universe continues on and on.

To clear the gap between yours, mine and ours the only thing required is intention to do so. That is why UR>. We, as part of the Divine, create by emotional thought. This book's sole goal is truly to clear the gap. Intending an Original Restoration of the All in All. Even if this is pie in the sky thinking, perhaps we can try. Restoring our computers/lifes to the day they were new is the implication here. What would happen if we intended this? Perhaps a cleared gap would offer a clear playing field to begin again. Who knows? I figure poofing the gap could not hurt and could offer spectacular miracles. How do you feel about this?

Chapter 6

See the best in a framed image by creating it in a text message

Watch it become an internal virtual movie of whatever it represents to you. See it with your internal eyes. Jump into that virtual movie. See it, feel it, do it and take back the memory of doing it your way. You then have a blueprint of the world from your inside mind to use in your outside world. Know that it is not what happens to you; it is how you choose to see it and react to it. We each know of people who have survived awful things and not only survived, but also thrived. Be that person. See a better situation. Create framed images of all kinds to visualize it clearer and clearer. You are writing your own life's script. If you do not like Act 1, rewrite Act 2.

You are more than just an actor in this world. You are the writer, director, props person, and cleanup crew.

Go to it.
Lights.
Camera.
Action!

What is it you want in your life? See it clearly in a framed image.

Try using snapshots, sketches, drafts, magazine images or online downloads.

The main idea here is to create wonderful things in your life. What you think about comes about, so be careful what you think about. Gratitude is the best thing to think of because thoughts are like boomerangs, they come right back to the sender.

[:)] U. R. Moore

Try these text images.
Create your own.
Share and pass on your ideas and creations.

Put each item into a frame of *[ ]*.
The frame is
[ ]
and the fireworks are the
*

on either side of the frame.

For example * [:)] * intends see the best, poof the rest, always with a smile of gratitude.

!

Intend for a bit more drama in
a life full of stagnation.

@

Intend a new point to be at in your life.
Perhaps a new
move,
job
or
goal.

$

Intend money to flow into your life,
with intention to share it.
Think of money as energy.
Without flowing,
it stagnates.

%

Ask for guidance of how much to give in
time,
energy
or
money.
Ask and listen in quiet,
like an echo,
it will come to you.

∧

Request Higher guidance,
wisdom,
and
understanding
of all kinds.

[:)] U. R. Moore

Intend inclusion,
release exclusion.
Intend to release judgments of all kinds.

Poof the rest.
Always smile with gratitude.

( )

This is my favorite. I use this for a global refresh button. This is much like the refresh button on your computer. The intention is a refresh of the globe with what is best for all concerned. My goal is not to impose what I see as the best. My intention is allowing everyone his or her own sweet dreams, lessons and drama, while I enjoy mine. This is the law of allowing Abraham Hicks voices. For free downloads see

Abrahamhicks.com.

||

Think of this as your inner tube of Light. Breathe in White Light from above and below, joining at the heart. Think of above as Divine Light and below as the Light of Mother Earth. Then see your heart fill with this Light and radiate out, cleansing every cell of your being. For a more information, see

Masteringalchemy.com.

This is amazing as a meditation while walking.

//

Intend a break out.
Break out of old ways,
bad situations,
difficult relationships,
old habits.
Intend to break out
of
anything
with the ease
of breaking out of an old paper bag.
See it.
Feel it.
Do it.
Smile in gratitude.

" "

Ask for a better way
to say
or
present something.

[:)] U. R. Moore

⁘

Intend seeing things
in
a
new,
clearer,
and
better light.

)

Gratitude.
If what you think about comes about,
thinking about
gratitude
brings more of what you are most grateful
for
right back into your life.
This is the best
energy boomerang effect possible.

THIS ONE CONCEPT IS HUGE!

< >

Intend filling the gap.
What is missing in your life?
Ask
and
you will be shown.
Watch for
coincidences of all kinds.

???

Here one might be asking for guidance.
Who,
what,
where,
when,
how
are some of the specific questions.

~

Ask for guidance to adjust. I truly believe that we have free will here. I further believe that if we do ask, multitudes of unseen helpers are at our disposal. If we refuse to ask for their help, I see them standing around with dusty wings, just waiting and waiting. So ask for help to adjust. Then listen and you will receive messages in dreams, music and coincidences. Adjusting to me is like being water. Water is life that flows downstream without effort. It will flow around rocks, over boulders, through canyons. It is strong enough to create the Grand Canyon, and gentle enough to sooth a baby. It refreshes and adjusts as needed. Ask to adjust, bend and flow like a river.

~ {} ~

This is my image of an angel.
It is so powerful when clearly pictured
that you can literally put your hand on it
and feel the presence of your own guardian
angel.
If you wish to see an angel painted by a
clairvoyant, go to pranichealing.com

{}

Intend to see a
door of opportunity
and have the
courage
to walk through it.
Ask for the key
if you feel
locked in
or
out
of a situation.

) (

This is my symbol to make it so.
After seeing my virtual movie clearly with
my inner eye,
my simple words are,
make it so.
Believe it or not,
the universe obeys our every command.

■

This is an image of a pause.
Pause and think.
Pause and ask for guidance.
Pause to use each moment to help anyone,
anytime,
anywhere
by intending a clearing of all dirty energy
around him or her.
So simple.
So powerful.

Use each moment to help
anyone,
anytime,
anywhere.

Try these pictures also:

Now be an armchair hero. Offer unseen help from wherever you are. Offer clearing of all dirty energy. Smile.

Intend an Original restoration.

Intend clearing the gap between yours *[:)]*, mine*[:)]* and ours *[:)]**[:)]*. Clear the gap because (UR>) you are more than just what you see here. Include asking for help from ~ {} ~.

Intend clearing all dirty energies presented in daily news broadcasts.

Whom could it hurt?

Could it help?

See crystal-clear bodies of water. See a pond, lake, or waterfall with clean waters flowing. Intend purification. Intend cleaning our physical oceans, lands and sky.

See the smog lift in any area, leaving clean air and clear vistas.

Put a special child's image, or any child to represent all children, and intend children's health and safety in all ways.

See food in abundance. See a field of grain or a fruit orchard, with enough food for all.

If you can see it, you can manifest it. See any new vision with intention for it to happen in a way that is best for all.

Intend peace, joy and happiness by using a simple smile of gratitude.

Poof ahead of you. Poof behind you. Poof all around you. Then visualize before yourself a carpet of flower pedals. Walk in joy and dignity. Leave a trail of pedals for others to walk on.

Observe what you give away, for only that is what you truly own.

See a chain either joining in joy or opening a link to release.

See a union, marriage or partnership as a shining of two stars so bright they appear as one.

Some of
my favorite images
include,
but
are
not
limited to

ANGELS WITH DUSTY WINGS
(FREE WILL AND ALL THAT JAZZ)

We have many unseen helpers. These helpers will not interfere with our lives without asking for their help. We come here with free will and unless and until we ask for help, we will not receive it. Your angels will wait as long as needed, while their wings get dusty. All you have to do is ask. They will wait for you.

CUP OVERFLOWING

This is classic. This may be pure joy that my life is full, or a request to the universe to have my life overflow with this joy.

The opposite of this image works well also. See an empty cup. For me it implies being open, ready to receive answers in the echo, or in the quietness.

There was a story about a student in search of wisdom who found a very wise monk. The monk poured tea into the student's cup and continued pouring to overflowing. The student protested, and the monk replied.

"This is like coming in search of wisdom, but not emptying the mind enough to accept the wisdom."

For me this image is a request to empty the non-helpful stuff in my mind to allow for the helpful wisdom.

DANCING

Dance is a physical expression of joy and a very healing image. When using an image for healing, always see the person dancing. See them spinning to the right, absorbing pure joy from the universe. I especially love to see them dancing on a beach, with a big floppy hat, spinning like a child laughing.

DOORS

See doors of all kinds, shapes, with and without keys, bars, windows, etc. They represent opportunities to me. I see new vistas, new places, and new people in my life through these doors. Some I can help, others help me.

Joel Osteen gives a great talk on walking through doors. See JoelOsteen.com. for free downloads.

The Bible says knock and it will be open to you.

A Course in Miracles talks about how the door left ajar for you, but you need to walk through it by your own choice.

An important dream of mine years ago was walking through a house made of doors, only doors. In order to get through the house I had to choose a door, then another, then another.

EMPTY VASE

This is classic also.
If you come to the Divine as an empty vase
with the intention to fill yourself with
positive White Light,
you are requesting powerful blessings,
insights,
guidance
and
abundance
of all kinds.

FEATHER ON THE HEART

Thinking of a
feather on the heart
can be an expression of
joy and happiness.
Goldie Hawn said
she was so happy all the time
that it was as if she was born
with a feather tickling her heart.
I love this image
and use it to ask for
joy in my life.

GENIE

This is a powerful image for me.
My world now revolves around the
concept that my
every emotional thought,
word,
and
deed
literally create.
I can hear the genie say,
"Your wish is my command."
This keeps me focused to
stay in the positive,
put no energy into the negative,
and ask only for wisdom to know the
difference.
I become aware that the
genie listens
to my every emotional thought,
not just the ones I think I would like.

GPS

I think of this as a
Global Peace System
or
God's Poofing System.
Either one works for me.
See the absolute best this globe could be.
Smile with gratitude
and
poof all the rest.
Let go of
all the doubt,
fear
and
anger.
The final snapshot
now has a new playing field all around it.
Now
new solutions
are
possible.

HANDS OF LIGHT

The image of being in the hands of the Divine
is
very healing.
For any healing request,
see the image of the loved one
resting comfortably in Hands of Light.
Intend healing of all kind.
Trust it is so.
Then let go.
Remember that the healing is not always
within our time period.
Smile
and
say thank you.
For energy healing classes
check out Pranichealing.com.

LEAVES FALLING

This helps to see that the natural cycle of death
is a blessing
not a problem.
How would your life change
if there were
no fear of death?
Please write me and let me know.
I would appreciate it.

LEAVING A TRAIL

We leave a trail of energy as we
move through this life.
It is not a question of if we do.
It is only an option of what kind of energy we
choose to leave behind.
Use the Rose to absorb and disintegrate all
negative energy around yourself.
This clears the path ahead of you
and
leaves a clearer path behind you.

MOUNTAIN

A mountain is a classic image of power.
See the image of a mountain
represent any problem.
Watch it spin to the right
and see the dirty energy fly off and
disintegrate.
My first experience with this image had
results within the hour.
The conflict
just resolved and never refocused.
Try it and please let me know your results.

PIE OF LIFE AND ALLOWING

Abrahamhicks.com has a fantastic free download on this. In short, it talks about the human experience as a well-stocked kitchen and each life is making a pie. The only way ingredients get into our pie is with emotional thought. If I am upset because you are putting pepper in your pie that pepper, goes into my pie by my own emotional thought of attention. Of course if you are making chicken potpie and I am making a fruit pie, our ingredients are different. Mind my own business equates to, "I will create my pie to bake, and you create your own."

PUPPIES

For me this is pure
fun,
joy
and
childhood wonder.
The smile just comes to my lips at the image.
No direction required.

ROSE

Using a single mystic rose, see it float all around you as it collects any dirty energy. See the pedals go from closed to open as it absorbs all dirty energy from even the root of any issue. Then see it burst into fireworks disintegrating all the collected dirty energy. Multiple roses are a relationship image for me. Sometimes it is impossible to know the words to ask for when wishing the best for all concerned. The relationship(s) can be beyond my understanding. The roses, like the hope for the relationship, are healthy, beautiful and with long stems. John Edward says if there are thornes on them, it represents a difficulty in the relationship. Then see the best and poof the rest*. The intention is to clear the playing field of everything and anything non-helpful for each individual concerned. See Masteringalchemy.com for a free DVD and other free mp3 downloads.

SHINING SUN

The Sun shows me
non-judgmental blessings.
It shines on all,
without
exceptions.
When I catch myself stuck in
how to see
the best in a bad situation,
this Sun image helps me
refocus.

SIGN AT THE DOOR OF GOD

All are welcome:
The good
and
the not so good.
This helps me curb my judgments of others.

SMILE WITHIN A HEART

Sometimes this is
the simplest image of joy I can think of.
It works for me.
How about you?

STADIUM SEATING WITH
CARDS ON EACH SEAT

As each person holds up the card left on his
or her seat,
a total image appears.
What this says to me is that the
Divine sets up the cards.
Each life represents one seat.
Until we put all the cards back to their
original placement,
we cannot successfully complete this
original design of life.

WHITE BUBBLE OF PROTECTION

During a very difficult time in my life, this image became salvation. Not only did it represent to me a bubble of protection around myself, it also represented putting my problems into bubbles and letting them float away. My neighbors must have thought me crazy for a time. Every afternoon I would sit on my porch with a bottle of child's bubbles and for hours on end, blow bubbles. My porch looked like a bubble machine. What went on in my mind was the image of each problem floated away in each bubble. What took hours was repeating this as often as needed. The great part is when the bubbles burst. Poof ... all gone. A virtual game that is now the stuff of my life.

I especially love this last image.
It is the commercial of the
duck, "Om'ing"
and the
cow, "Mooing."
See youtube.com the Cali Milk Commercial.
A duck is doing meditation with repeating,
"Om."
A cow comes along and corrects the duck
saying,
"It is not Om, but Moo."

What a delight to watch.
It keeps my mind clear that I know
I do not know.
Who am I to judge?
My request then is, "Please show me."

Chapter 7.

This idy bid e universal
bubble of ours.

What if our universal image is:

[:)] ~ {} ~ [ur]> ~ {} ~ *[:)]* ~ {} ~

[ur]> ~ {} ~ *[:)]* ~ {} ~ [ur]> ~ {} ~

within a bubble that looks like O?

What if our understanding grew to
acknowledge that we are in
one universal bubble
surrounded by
many,
many
other universal bubbles?

O

O O

O O
O we are here,
in this idy bid e universal bubble
surrounded by many other universes.

Perhaps each universal bubble is only one wave of the total Divine Ocean. Would it then be possible to imagine how vast all of creation is?

Each single soul is still more than we know. Each soul is still a spiritual being on a magnificent human journey. However, perhaps now we can pause just long enough to ask and listen in quiet for some direction from our unseen helpers just waiting for our call. Perhaps we can pause before we rearrange the stadium cards without the Divine direction.

Moreover, maybe, just maybe, we can lighten up; keep it simple, and SEE THE BEST, POOF THE REST. Who knows?

So now

[:)] ~ {} ~ [ur]> ~ {} ~ *[:)]* ~ {} ~

[ur]> ~ {} ~ *[:)]* ~ {} ~ [ur]> ~ {} ~ with unseen helpers all around us in a Divine Ocean wave that goes on and on within our universe.

ONCE AGAIN...

Taking this image changes it to look like an O surrounded by many other O's and it blends into what may look like this:

O

O   O

O   O

O we are here, in this idy bid e universal bubble surrounded by many other universes. We are a Divine Ocean in our own universe, but a Divine Ocean wave in the totality of universes. All the universes are part of the Divine Ocean. Each universe is a Divine Ocean wave. Each one soul is so important that without you there is a void in the All in All of universes. Wow. OK. Got it?

It is great if you get it because this is the fun part. However, the bottom line really is its ok if you did not get it. You are exactly where you need to be at any given time.

Smile.
You are loved,
watched over,
and have unseen helpers
at your disposal.
Smile.
Than
Smile
again.

Please send us feedback on this book.
Let us know your favorite images and ideas.

What are the changes in your life?

How do you see yourself now?
Can you see ur>?

Can you see others are more than they think
also?

Does that change your world, inside and out,
at all?

My Dearest Reader,

May your life be filled with
whatever makes your heart smile.
It maybe joy, peace and love.
Nevertheless, it also maybe dramas,
the stuff of life as you know it.
The ultimate game plan question is,
"Can I have joy, peace and love,
while you enjoy the drama of it all?"

Let the games begin,
consciously this time.
Enjoy!

Visit us at URMoore-books.com
[:)]
We welcome your comments and insights.
URMoore.books@yahoo.com

Acknowledgements

No book gets published without help,
and I am grateful for the talented
work of the following people:

Marie Cirillo
for editing and illustration

Trent Dyar, Design Consultant
for coordinating the production of this book

Casey Reuter, Cover Designer
for work on the cover

Alison McCartney, Book Designer
for work on the interior layout

AuthorHouse Author Support Team
for being professional and easy to talk to